Y4Y 3'85

The Ladybird Key Words Reading Scheme is based on these commonly used words. Those used most often in the English language are introduced first—with other words of popular appeal to children. All the Key Words list is covered in the early books, and the later titles use further word lists to develop full reading fluency. The total number of different words which will be learned in the complete reading scheme is nearly two thousand. The gradual introduction of these words, frequent repetition and complete 'carry-over' from book to book, will ensure rapid learning.

The full-colour illustrations have been designed to create a desirable attitude towards learning—by making every child *eager* to read each title. Thus this attractive reading scheme embraces not only the latest findings in word frequency, but also the natural interests and activities of happy children.

Each book contains a list of the new words introduced.

W. MURRAY, the author of the Ladybird Key Words Reading Scheme, is an experienced head-master, author and lecturer on the teaching of reading. He is co-author, with J. McNally, of 'Key Words to Literacy'—a teacher's book published by The Schoolmaster Publishing Co. Ltd.

For use in schools. colourful supporting material and apparatus ba~~sed on the Words is available~~. W~~rite for~~ details

WILLS & HEH, Leics.

D1134331

THE LADYBIRD KEY WORDS READING SCHEME has 12 graded books in each of its three series—**'a'**, **'b'** and **'c'**. These 36 graded books are all written on a controlled vocabulary, and take the learner from the earliest stages of reading to reading fluency.

The **'a'** series gradually introduces and repeats new words. The parallel **'b'** series gives the needed further repetition of these words at each stage, but in different context and with different illustrations.

The **'c'** series is also parallel to the **'a'** series, and supplies the necessary link with writing and phonic training.

An illustrated booklet—'Notes for Teachers' —can be obtained free from the publishers. This booklet fully explains the Key Words principle and the Ladybird Key Words Reading Scheme. It also includes information on the books and apparatus available, and such details as the vocabulary loading and reading ages of all books.

Book 8b

THE LADYBIRD KEY WORDS
READING SCHEME

The big house

by
W. MURRAY

with illustrations by
MARTIN AITCHISON

Publishers: Wills & Hepworth Ltd., Loughborough
First published 1966   ©   Printed in England

This morning there are some letters for Peter, Jane and their Daddy. The children like to get letters from their friends. Their mother and father help them to read some of these letters, but some others they can read on their own.

Today Jane is glad to see she has a letter from her Aunty. Jane and Peter were at Aunty's house for their summer holiday. Aunty writes to thank Jane for her letter and to say that she and Uncle are well.

Peter is glad to have a letter from his friend Jack. Jack is a big boy who lives by the sea. Peter can read some of his letter, but not all of it.

The two children go into the house. "There is a letter for you," calls Peter to his father. He puts his father's letter on the table.

The brother and sister tell their mother about the letters. She helps Jane to read some of her letter from Aunty and Uncle, and then helps Peter with his letter from his friend Jack.

Father opens his letter and reads it as he sits at the table. It is a long letter from an old friend. He takes a long time to read the letter. Then he looks up to tell the others about it.

"I have an old friend who has a very big house," he says. "His name is Mr White. He has a very big garden by his house. This old friend has to go away from his home until Christmas. He wants us to look after his house and garden when he is away. There are some birds and rabbits and fish in the garden. We would have to look after these as well as the flowers."

"What fun," says Peter. "We would love to help you to look after Mr White's house and garden."

"It is a long time until Christmas," says Mother.

"We could do it," says Jane. "We would all be glad to help."

"He says you two children could play in the garden," says Daddy.

"That is good of him," says Mother.

Mother and Father talk some more about Mr White's letter. Then they tell the children that they are going to look after Mr White's house and garden until Christmas, as he asks.

"You will have to help with the work," Mother says to them.

After dinner Father says he is going to write a letter to Mr White. He gets a pen and some ink and sits down at the table. Peter sits at the table with him. He does not use pen and ink, as he wants to draw. He draws with pencils. Peter uses red, blue, green and yellow pencils to make a picture of a garden.

"I have never been to Mr White's garden," says Peter. "Is it like this, Daddy?"

His father puts the pen and ink away and looks at Peter's picture. "I like your picture," he says, "but Mr White's garden is a big one. Let me use your pencils to draw it for you."

He takes Peter's pencils and draws. Then he says, "Have a look at this."

The summer weather is not over. It is a lovely time of the year. The sun is out, but it is not too hot.

Both the children are out with their father and mother. They are going to the shops. Peter has his father's letter in his hand. He looks at it and tells Jane that he can read the name on it.

Jane and her mother go into a hat shop. Mother wants to buy a new hat. As his mother and sister go into the shop Peter tells his father that he thinks they will be a long time.

"We have plenty to do," says Father. "First we must send off the letter and then get some things for the garden."

"It is just the weather to work in the garden," says Peter. "We will give you plenty of help at Mr White's house."

Peter and his father go in and out of the shops for a long time, until they have all they want. Then they go to find Mother and Jane.

Mr White,
THE GABLES,
SEAFORD,
SUSSEX

Father and Peter have to wait some time for Mother and Jane. Then Peter says, "I can see them now. Here they are."

Mother has bought a new hat. "I hope you like the hat I have bought," she says.

"I like it," says Peter. "You have found a nice one."

"Yes, you have picked a nice one," says Father. "I think it is lovely. We both like it."

Mother looks happy. "A woman always likes a new hat," she says. "I have not bought another hat this year."

"We had to wait a long time," Peter says to Jane. "It made me think you were lost."

"When are we going to see the big garden?" asks Jane. "Can we go today?"

Father says, "We have too much to do today. We will go over in two days' time. I put that in my letter to Mr White. I want to see him before he goes away. We should have a talk before he goes. Come on now, it is five o'clock and time to go home."

Today, Mother, Father and the children are going by car to see Mr White and his house and garden. It is a sunny day.

"What beautiful weather," says Mother, as she gets into the car.

"Yes," says Father, "it is a lovely day to go out in the car." He tells the children the way that they will go.

Soon the car is going fast along the road. It goes up over the hill and then down by the woods. After this it goes by the farm.

The children look out of the windows of the car and talk. "There is the donkey," says Peter.

"Yes, the dear old donkey," says Jane. "We must go and see him soon."

Then they come to Mr White's house. The car stops by a door in a wall. The door is closed. "This is the garden door," says Father.

It is a lovely sunny wall. It is yellow, and there are flowers on the top of the wall. Some beautiful butterflies are by the flowers.

"I love butterflies," says Jane.

Father and Mother go round to the other door to see Mr White. Peter and Jane wait in the car by the door in the yellow wall. They look at the wall and at the lovely blue flowers and the butterflies.

The garden door has PRIVATE on it. "Can you read what is on the door?" Peter asks Jane. "Yes, it is PRIVATE," she says.

"I can read PRIVATE, too," says Peter. "It means people can go in only if they want to see Mr White."

"Yes," says Jane, "PRIVATE means that the door and the garden are for his use only."

The door is closed, but soon they can hear some people in the garden. Then the door opens and they hear their father call.

Peter and Jane push the car door open, jump out, and go in the garden door.

There are their father and mother with Mr White. "This is Mr White," says Father, " and here are Peter and Jane."

Mr White tells the children he is glad they want to help with the garden.

Mr White wants them to see his garden. Peter and Jane and their mother have not been there before.

"Come round with me," he says, "I am always happy to take people round my garden. Then you must come into the house for a cup of tea before you go back."

He talks to them as he takes them round. They all stop to look at the fruit trees.

"We have had a lot of fruit this year," Mr White says. "We have picked some, but there is a lot more to pick, as you can see. Do you like to pick fruit, Peter and Jane?"

"Yes, we do," says Peter.

"I would be glad if you could pick some of this," says Mr White. "The last time I went away the fruit was left on the trees. You may eat as much as you like, and take some home with you."

"Thank you," says Peter, "we could make some jam with it. We all like jam."

"Yes, and I know how to make jam," says Jane.

They go on round the garden, and come to a very big rabbit run. The children look for the rabbits.

"There are not many here," says Jane, "I can see only three."

"I can see the heads of two more. Look over there," says Peter.

"Some of them hide when people come to see them," says Mr White. "If you came at night and could see, there would be a lot of them out."

"It is a good place to keep rabbits," says Peter, "they have room to run about."

"Yes, there is plenty of room," says Mr White, "but three of them got out last week."

"Did any get lost ? Did you get them back?" asks Peter. "No, they were not lost," says Mr White, " but it was like a game of hide-and-seek to get them back. I did get them in the end, but I got wet as there was rain at the time."

The children want to make friends with the rabbits and they bring them something to eat.

Many fish are in the water. Peter and Jane can see a lot of them as they swim about. Peter puts his hand into the water and one of the fish swims up to it.

"Look, Jane," says Peter, "I think this big red and black fish wants something to eat."

"Don't fall in," says Mother to Peter.

"He did fall in some water once," Jane tells Mr White. "We had to pull him out. His clothes got very wet."

"Never again," says Peter. "I am not going to fall in again."

"I am glad to hear that," says his mother, "we have no other clothes with us."

"I would like to watch these fish for a long time," says Jane, "I think they are beautiful."

"There is a book about fish at school," says Peter. "I had a look at it last week. There were pictures in it of fish just like these."

"You can learn a lot from books," says Mr White. "I have many books about fish, flowers, rabbits, birds and gardens."

"Here are my birds," says Mr White.

"You have a lot of very beautiful birds," says Mother. "I think there is nothing more beautiful than a lovely bird."

"I like to hear a bird sing first thing in the morning as I get up," says Father. "It makes me happy."

"When I hear a bird sing, it makes me want to sing, too," says Jane.

They can see that Mr White loves his birds. He gives them some water to drink. The birds know him and some of them come to him. One bird is on his hand and another is on his head.

"I do not want to go away from them," he says. "I think about my little friends when I am away. I am glad to know you will look after them well, for me."

"We will give them plenty to eat and drink," says Peter.

"We had better have a cup of tea now," says Mr White. "You can all come along with me up to the house."

They all have seats by the windows where they can look down on the garden.

The children have ice-creams and the others have tea to drink.

"It is like a café up here," says Peter.

Mr White says, "I like nothing better than to sit here after dinner, in good weather. I come out here every day when the sun is out. I can see a lot from here."

There is a black and red butterfly by the flowers on the table. Peter and Jane both watch it fly about. Then it goes away. "Let it fly away," says Mother, "it is happy in the sun."

Mr White and Mother and Father want to talk for some time, so Mr White asks the children if they would like to go and play in the garden. "You could play hide-and-seek or some other game," he says.

Peter and Jane want to look round the garden again. "There is so much to do here," says Jane. "Yes," says Peter, "let us go and look at those fish again."

Peter and Jane have found some balls in a box. "I know the game to play with these," says Peter. "People play it in the park."

"Yes," says Jane, "I know children play this game in the park. I saw them once. Let us play it now. We can learn how to do it."

They look up at Mr White and ask him if they can use the balls for a game.

"Yes," says Mr White, "go on. Have some fun. We can watch you play from here."

The children take some balls out of the box to play the game. Peter hits his ball. Then Jane hits hers. At first they are not very good at it and one of the balls is lost by some logs. They find it and then go on with the game. They get better at it as they play.

"I like this," says Peter, "but not as much as cricket. Some people say cricket is a slow game, but I do not think it is slow."

Mr White went away last week. Peter and his father are at work in the garden. There has been some bad weather and it has made a lot of work in the garden.

Peter is under a tree as he picks up some apples. Not many apples have come down from the tree. Peter picks them up and puts them in a box. He can see his father at work.

A little apple falls from the tree and hits Peter on the head. He looks up and sees the cat in the tree. He calls the cat down and takes it to the house to give it something to eat.

He talks to the cat. "This is your dinner," he says. "That's right, eat it up." The cat eats its dinner and then has a drink.

Peter goes back to get the box of apples. He takes it to an old stable at the end of the garden. Mr White keeps his car in the old stable when he is at home. The car is not in the stable now.

Peter and Jane are in the old stable. There is a room over the stable and Peter wants to get into it.

"I know how to get into that room," he says. "Come on, Jane, let us have a look round up there. It will be fun."

The two children get into the room. Jane opens a window so that they can see.

There is a big black box in the room. "What can be in there?" asks Peter. "I wish we could open the box and see what is in it."

He goes over to the box and has a look at it. "We can open it, Jane," he says. "Help me to look in here."

They find a tent, some old pictures, a top hat and a cricket bat and cap. Peter takes out the cricket bat and the cricket cap.

Jane looks at the pictures. "Here is one of an old Queen," she says. "It is our Queen's grandmother."

Peter takes out the top hat and puts it on. "Look, Jane," he says.

Peter and Jane have fun dressing up in the room over the stable. All children like dressing up.

Then they go into the house. They want to see Mr White's books. "He said we must see the books," says Peter. "I know where they are," says Jane. "I know which room they are in."

They find the books in a sunny room at the top of the house.

"What a lot there are," says Peter. "Mr White must have a lot of money to buy all these." "Some may have been presents," says Jane. "Many people give books for presents."

They sit down in two chairs to look at some of the books. Jane has a book about butterflies. "Look at this beautiful butterfly on this log," she says to Peter. "It is yellow and black."

Peter has a book about fish. "There are some fish here like those Mr White has," he says. "I could learn a lot about fish from these pictures."

The children find books about horses, motor cars, birds and flowers.

The children tell their father about Mr White's books. Peter says he saw a very old book with Punch and Judy in it. "I did not know they had Punch and Judy in those days," says Jane.

"Yes," says Father, "Punch and Judy are very old. I saw them when I was a boy, and so did your Grandfather."

"Have you left the books just as you found them?" asks Father. "Yes," says Jane, "we put all the books back again."

As they talk the two children help their father work in the garden. He tells them he wants to make a fire and looks round for a place for it. "It must be away from the birds and the trees and the rabbits," he says.

Then they find a good place for a fire. Peter likes to make a fire. He brings some wood for his father to put on it.

Jane says, "Mummy saw Pam's mother the other day. She says our friend Jack wants to come to the farm for a holiday."

Jack has come to Pam's farm for two weeks' holiday. He has a friend with him. When Peter and Jane were on their own holiday by the sea they used to talk to Jack about Pam's farm and about the good times they had there. It made Jack want to go to the farm for a holiday.

Jack and his friend have come in a van. It is Jack's uncle's van. They have a tent in it. Pam's father tells them where they can put their tent.

There are some logs by the barn. Pam's father tells the boys they can make a log house if they want to.

Peter and Jane come up to the farm to see Jack. They talk to him about the happy days they had by the sea. "I used to like going on the pier to fish," says Peter. "Yes, and I liked picnics on the sands," says Jane.

They talk about the day they lost their kite and how Jack and his friend helped them to find it.

Jack and his friend have been at the farm for some days now and they like it very much. They live in their tent. There has been no bad weather.

The two boys help on the farm. They like to work out in the sun with Pam's father and his men.

Peter and Jane come up to the farm again to see their friends. They ask them to make a log house.

"Why?" asks Jack. "For us to play in," says Jane. "Go on, it would be fun. We would help you."

Jack and his friend like to please Peter and Jane, so they say they will make them a log house.

First, Jack looks at the logs and thinks. Then he says, "I know how to do it. Help me to push those big ones over here."

Pam's black puppy comes up to see what is going on. He wants to play. "No," says Jane to the puppy, "we have work to do." Some little chicks come by and the puppy runs off after them.

Jack and his friend make the log house for the children. They find an old door and put it into place.

Jane wants the boys to know that she can write. She writes ENTRANCE WAY IN on the door. When he sees this, Peter writes EXIT WAY OUT.

Pam comes along. "Has my puppy been here?" she asks. "Yes," says Jane. "He came by here and then ran off to play with some chicks. He ran that way. I will come with you to help find him if you like."

Peter talks to Jack. He says, "You can swim very well and I like the way you dive into the water. I want to learn to dive like you. I can swim a little now."

Jack says, "If you want to swim well, swim every day if you can. I live by the sea, so I can swim every day."

Jane comes back. "Pam has found her puppy," she says. She plays in the log house with Peter until it is time to go home.

ENTRANCE

WAY

IN

Peter asks Jack to take him for a swim. "I want to see you dive," he says.

Jack asks his friend if he would like to go for a swim. "Yes," says his friend, "it has been very hot today. It would be nice to get into the water."

"Come on," says Jack. "Let us get our things from the tent, and then Peter will tell us the way to go."

They get into the van and go along the road. Then they get out and walk a little way. They talk as they go along. Peter tells his friends how he fell off a tree the other day and sat in the water. "When I fell off I had my clothes on. It is fun to talk about it now," he says, "but as I sat in the water I did not like it."

Soon the boys are by the water. Jack dives in. As he goes under the water Peter thinks, "I must learn to dive like that."

Then Jack helps Peter to dive.

The three boys like it in the water very much. Jack can swim well and so can his friend. They see that Peter does not get into danger.

One of the boys finds a big log in the water. "We can have some fun with this," he says.

Jack gets on the log, but he soon falls off as it goes over and over in the water. When he falls off Jack goes under the water again. Then his friend gets on the log and Jack and Peter push him along.

"Let us see if all three of us can sit on the log at once," says Jack. "I will help Peter get up on to it."

Peter gets up on the log. "Now help me," says Jack. The other two pull him up, but the log goes over again and they all three fall into the water.

They play some more and then at last Jack says that it is time to go back.

They stop at a shop on the way back to buy some ice-cream.

The boys play a game of cricket by the barn. Jack is by the wall with the bat. His friend has the ball first, and then Peter has it.

Jack hits the ball and runs. He makes a lot of runs.

Jane looks on. "Jack can play well," she says. "He hits the ball all over the place. It is going up over the trees now."

Then Jack hits the ball again. It goes over the barn.

"The ball may be lost," calls his friend. "We must all go to find it." They all go round the barn to find the ball.

A man from the farm is at work there. The puppy is with him. "I saw your ball come over the barn," he says, "I think it is over there by the pigs." Peter runs over and finds it. Then they all go back to the game. The puppy is with them.

Peter has the bat now. Every time he hits the ball the puppy runs after it. The puppy likes to play with children.

It has been lovely weather all day. There has been no rain and the sun has been out all the time. It has been hot.

Now the sun is down and the night has come. Peter and Jane are at home in bed.

"It is going to be a beautiful night," says Jack, "but I do not want to go to bed now."

"Let us make a log fire," says his friend. "Then I will play and we will both sing."

"Yes," says Jack, "come on, then."

They make a big fire of logs. The fire is yellow and red and the trees look black. The boys sit by the fire and Jack sings as his friend plays. Then they both sing.

The boys sing of danger at sea in bad weather. They sing about the woods in the summer time, and about a man and his horse.

In the farm house Pam's father and mother are going to bed. Their window is open and they can hear the boys sing. They like to hear them.

Words new to this book

Total number of words new to this book 91
The vocabulary of this book is the same
as that of the parallel reader 8a